everyday Vocabulary
Intervention Activities

M000266315

Table of Contents

Using Everyday Vocabulary Intervention Activities

Current research identifies vocabulary and word study as essential skills for reading success. Before children learn to read, they need to be aware of the meaning of words. Vocabulary instruction teaches children how to determine the meanings of words by utilizing contextual and conceptual clues. Word-study and word-solving strategies help children build their vocabularies, which leads to increased reading comprehension.

Effective vocabulary activities provide students with opportunities to:

- Actively engage in learning more about words and how words work

- Build their vocabularies and gain greater control of language

- Develop the ability to use context clues to define unfamiliar words

- Develop and build content vocabulary

Although some students master these skills easily during regular classroom instruction, many others need additional re-teaching opportunities to master these essential skills. The Everyday Vocabulary Intervention Activities series provides easy-to-use, five-day intervention units for Grades K–5. These units are structured around a research-based Model-Guide-Practice-Apply approach. You can use these activities in a variety of intervention models, including Response to Intervention (RTI).

Everyday Vocabulary Intervention Activities Grade K • ©2011 Newmark Learning, LLC

Getting Started

In just five simple steps, *Everyday Vocabulary Intervention Activities* provides everything you need to identify students' needs and to provide targeted intervention.

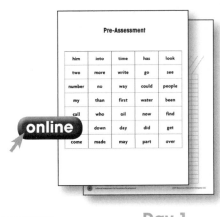

1. PRE-ASSESS to identify students' vocabulary needs.
Use the pre-assessment to identify the skills your students need to master.

2. MODEL the skill.
Every five-day unit targets a specific vocabulary and word study. On Day 1, use the teacher prompts and reproducible activity page to introduce and model the skill.

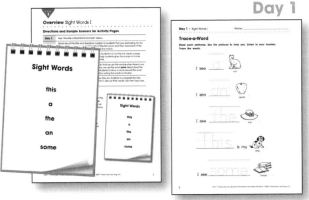

3. GUIDE, PRACTICE, and APPLY.
Use the reproducible practice activities for Days 2, 3, and 4 to build students' understanding and skill-proficiency.

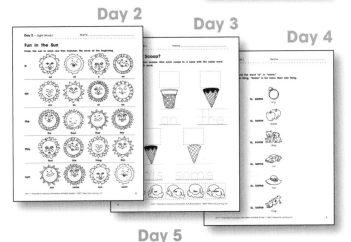

4. MONITOR progress.
Administer the Day 5 reproducible assessment to monitor each student's progress and to make instructional decisions.

5. POST-ASSESS to document student progress.
Use the post-assessment to measure students' progress as a result of your interventions.

Standards-Based Vocabulary Awareness
Skills in Everyday Intervention Activities

The vocabulary words and strategies found in the Everyday Intervention Activities series are introduced developmentally and spiral from one grade to the next. The chart below shows the types of words and skill areas addressed at each grade level in this series.

Everyday Vocabulary Intervention Activities Series Skills	K	1	2	3	4	5
Sight Words	✔	✔	✔	✔		
Nouns, Pronouns, and Proper Nouns	✔	✔	✔	✔	✔	✔
Verbs	✔	✔	✔	✔	✔	✔
Adjectives	✔	✔	✔	✔	✔	✔
Synonyms and Antonyms	✔	✔	✔	✔	✔	✔
Compound Words		✔	✔	✔	✔	✔
Multiple-Meaning Words	✔	✔	✔	✔	✔	✔
Classify Words by Subject	✔	✔	✔	✔	✔	✔
Word Analogies	✔	✔	✔	✔	✔	✔
Word Parts and Root Words	✔	✔	✔	✔	✔	✔
Word Webs and Diagrams	✔	✔	✔	✔	✔	✔
Using Words in Context	✔	✔	✔	✔	✔	✔
Using Context Clues to Determine Word Meaning				✔	✔	✔
English Language Arts Content Words	✔	✔	✔	✔	✔	✔
Social Studies Content Words	✔	✔	✔	✔	✔	✔
Science Content Words	✔	✔	✔	✔	✔	✔
Math Content Words	✔	✔	✔	✔	✔	✔

Using Everyday Intervention for RTI

According to the National Center on Response to Intervention, RTI "integrates assessment and intervention within a multi-level prevention system to maximize student achievement and to reduce behavior problems." This model of instruction and assessment allows schools to identify at-risk students, monitor their progress, provide research-proven interventions, and "adjust the intensity and nature of those interventions depending on a student's responsiveness."

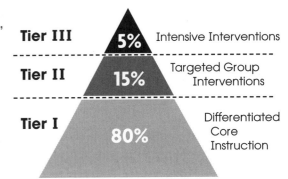

RTI models vary from district to district, but the most prevalent model is a three-tiered approach to instruction and assessment.

The Three Tiers of RTI	Using Everyday Intervention Activities
Tier I: Differentiated Core Instruction • Designed for all students • Preventive, proactive, standards-aligned instruction • Whole- and small-group differentiated instruction • Ninety-minute, daily core reading instruction in the five essential skill areas: phonics, phonemic awareness, comprehension, vocabulary, fluency	• Use whole-group vocabulary mini-lessons to introduce and guide practice with vocabulary strategies that all students need to learn. • Use any or all of the units in the order that supports your core instructional program.
Tier II: Targeted Group Interventions • For at-risk students • Provide thirty minutes of daily instruction beyond the ninety-minute Tier I core reading instruction • Instruction is conducted in small groups of three to five students with similar needs	• Select units based on your students' areas of need (the pre-assessment can help you identify these). • Use the units as week-long, small-group mini-lessons.
Tier III: Intensive Interventions • For high-risk students experiencing considerable difficulty in reading • Provide up to sixty minutes of additional intensive intervention each day in addition to the ninety-minute Tier I core reading instruction • More intense and explicit instruction • Instruction conducted individually or with smaller groups of one to three students with similar needs	• Select units based on your students' areas of need. • Use the units as one component of an intensive vocabulary intervention program.

Overview Sight Words I

Directions and Sample Answers for Activity Pages

Day 1	See "Provide a Real-World Example" below.
Day 2	Read aloud the title and directions. Explain to students that you are looking for the matching words. Help by reading aloud the first word, and then read each of the words below the suns. Guide them to find the match.
Day 3	Read aloud the title and directions. Help students cut out the ice cream scoops and name the word on each one. Then help students glue the scoops on cones with matching words, and repeat the words.
Day 4	Read aloud the title and directions. Explain that we use the word **a** when there is one of something. When there is more than one, we use the word **some**. Read aloud the two options for each phrase, and guide students to draw a circle around the word that is the right one. Allow them to practice writing the words on the line.
Day 5	Read aloud the title and directions. Allow time for students to complete the task. Afterward, meet individually with students to discuss their results. Use their responses to plan further instruction and review.

Provide a Real-World Example

- ◆ Write **this** and **a** on the board. Point to a book on the bookshelf. **Say:** *This is a book.* Write the words **this** and **a** on chart paper. Now point to a specific book on your desk. **Say:** *This is the book we will read today.* Write **the** on the chart paper.

- ◆ **Say:** *This, a,* and *the* are words we use all the time when we talk, write, and read.

- ◆ Hand out the Day 1 activity page. **Say:** *Let's look at more words we see and say all the time.* Read the first sentence aloud. Repeat the word **a**. **Say:** *Let's trace the word a.*

- ◆ Read the second sentence aloud. **Say:** *Let's trace the word an.* Repeat these steps with the rest of the sentences.

Trace-a-Word

Read each sentence. Use the pictures to help you. Listen to your teacher. Trace the words.

I see _____ a _____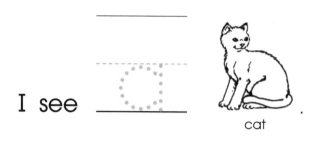
cat .

I see _____ an _____
apple .

I see _____ the _____
hat .

This is my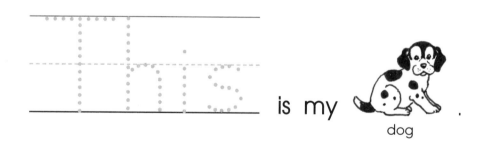
dog .

I see _____ some _____
books .

Unit 1 • Everyday Vocabulary Intervention Activities Grade K • ©2011 Newmark Learning, LLC

Fun in the Sun

Color the sun in each row that matches the word at the beginning.

a
   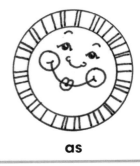

an   at   a   as

an

am   as   at   an

the

the   then   that   this

this

that   this   thing   thin

some

sun   some   son   soon

What's the Scoop?

Cut out the ice cream scoops. Glue each scoop to a cone with the same word below it. Trace each word.

Unit 1 • Everyday Vocabulary Intervention Activities Grade K • ©2011 Newmark Learning, LLC

Circle It!

We use the word "a" for one thing. We use the word "some" for more than one thing. Circle and write the word for each picture.

_____

- -

_____

a   **some**

hat

_____

- -

_____

a   **some**

apples

_____

- -

_____

a   **some**

dogs

_____

- -

_____

a   **some**

car

_____

- -

_____

a   **some**

frogs

Assessment

Draw a circle around the two words in each row that are the same.

a	as	a	an

a	an	an	at

the	this	that	the

this	the	this	that

same	some	seem	some

Overview Sight Words II

Directions and Sample Answers for Activity Pages

Day 1	See "Provide a Real-World Example" below.
Day 2	Read aloud the title and directions. Guide students to identify each picture as showing the concept of "in" or "out" and check the correct box. (out, in, in, out)
Day 3	Read aloud the title and directions. Help students identify each word and color it as instructed. (Mystery picture: flower)
Day 4	Read aloud the title and directions. Guide students to identify the word **to** in the path. Guide them to connect the path made up of the word **to**.
Day 5	Read aloud the title and directions. Allow time for students to complete the word find. Afterward, meet individually with students to discuss their results. Use their responses to plan further instruction and review.

Provide a Real-World Example

◆ Walk into the classroom and **say:** *I am walking into the classroom.* Then walk out of the classroom and say loudly from the hall: *Now I am out of the classroom.* Write the words **into** and **out** on chart paper.

◆ Put a book on your desk. **Say:** *The book is **on** the desk.* Add the word **on** to the chart paper. Place a ruler next to the book. **Say:** *The ruler is with the book.* Write **with** on the chart paper.

◆ **Say:** *into*, *out*, *on*, and *with* *are words that tell us where things are. They are called prepositions. We use prepositions all the time when we talk, write, and read.*

◆ Hand out the Day 1 activity page. **Say:** *The girl is **with** her dad in the kitchen. Let's trace the word **with**.* Draw attention to the ingredients on the table. **Say:** *The eggs are on the table. Let's trace the word **on**.* Allow students time to trace. Then **say:** *The girl is pouring oil into the bowl. Let's trace the word **into**.*

Sight Words

into

out

on

with

In the Kitchen with Dad

Trace each word. Write the words on the lines.

In or Out?

Look at each picture. Check the "IN" or "OUT" box to describe what you see.

	IN	OUT
(barrel and apple)	☐	☐
(hand pouring milk into cup)	☐	☐
(doghouse with dog)	☐	☐
(house and person walking)	☐	☐

Name _____

Mystery Picture

What do spring showers bring? Color the spaces with "at" yellow.
Color the spaces with "of" green. Color the spaces with "for" blue.

Henry Goes Home

Connect the stones with the word "to" to make a path from Henry to his home.

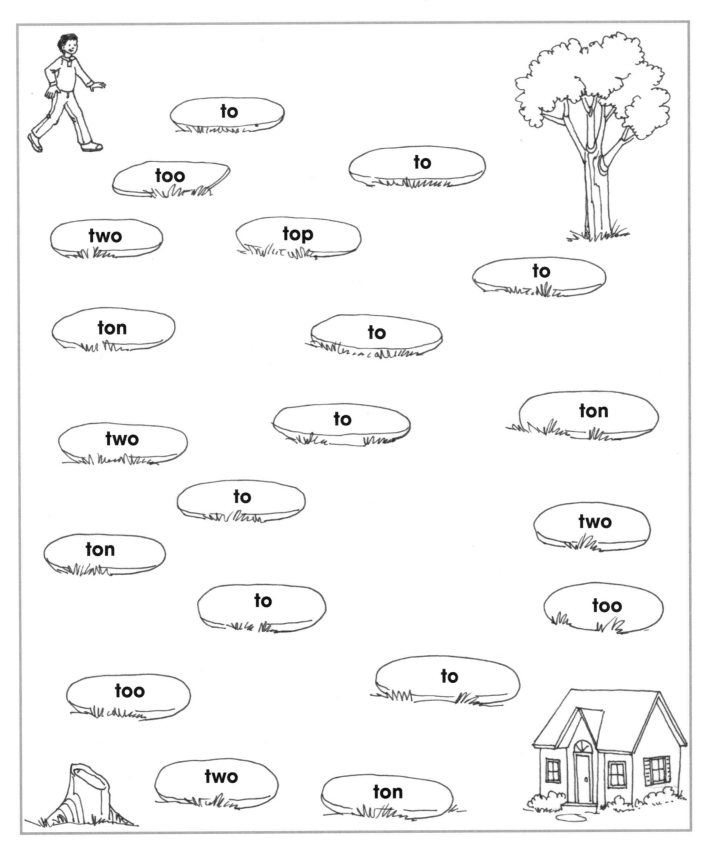

Name _____

Assessment

Find and circle the words from the box.

IN	ON	TO	INTO	OUT	WITH	FOR	OF

Word Find

```
C Z I N W R T O R O
Q B P C K A Y X E D
P O N H V H M O U T
F O R U O F M I R W
H U K F H Y C B J P
I N T O D P W I T H
```

Unit 2 • Everyday Vocabulary Intervention Activities Grade K • ©2011 Newmark Learning, LLC

Overview Sight Words III

Directions and Sample Answers for Activity Pages

Day 1	See "Provide a Real-World Example" below.
Day 2	Read aloud the title and directions. Help students match the words on the fish to the words in the air bubbles by drawing a line between them.
Day 3	Read aloud the title and directions. Divide the class into pairs. Describe how to play tic-tac-toe. Explain that instead of X and O, one partner is **yes** and the other is **no**. Help students cut out the words and guide as they play.
Day 4	Read aloud the title and directions. Help students identify the pictures. For each picture, ask if they need this item in the snow. If yes, help them glue it in the YES column. If no, help them glue it in the NO column. (YES: mittens, hat, snow boots; NO: swimsuit, beach ball, flip-flops)
Day 5	Read aloud the title and directions. Allow time for students to complete the first task. Then ask them to draw something they can do and label the box **Yes**. In the second box, they are to draw something they cannot do and label it **No**. Afterward, meet individually with students to discuss their results. Use their responses to plan further instruction and review.

Provide a Real-World Example

◆ Write the words **but** and **as** on chart paper. Point to the two words as you **say:** *I like vanilla ice cream, but not as much as I love chocolate!* Now write the word **too** on the chart paper. Point to the word as you **say:** *Strawberry is a good flavor, too.*

◆ **Say:** ***But**, **as**, and **too** are words we use all the time when we talk, write, and read.*

◆ Hand out the Day 1 activity page. **Say:** *Let's look at more words we see and say all the time.* Draw students' attention to the first sentence and read it aloud, emphasizing the word **or**: *I eat an apple or a banana. Repeat the word **or**. Let's trace the word **or**.*

◆ Read the second sentence, emphasizing the word **and**. **Say:** *I eat an apple and a banana. Repeat the word **and**. Let's trace the word **and**.* Repeat steps with the rest of the sentences.

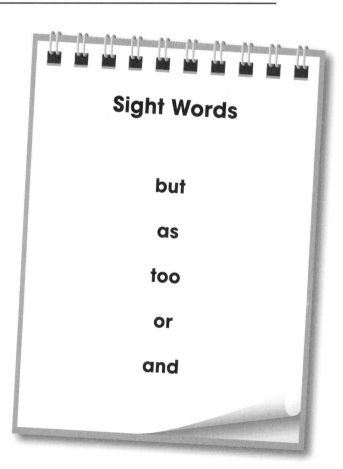

Sight Words

but

as

too

or

and

Apple and Banana

Read the sentences. Trace the words.

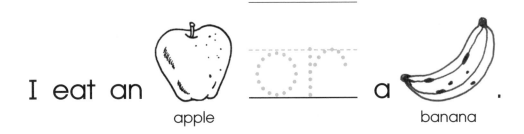

I eat an [apple] _or_ a [banana] .

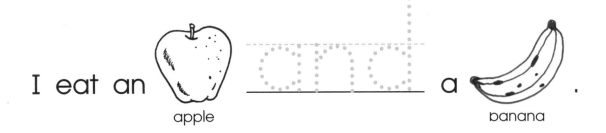

I eat an [apple] _and_ a [banana] .

I eat an [apple] . I eat a [banana] , _too_ .

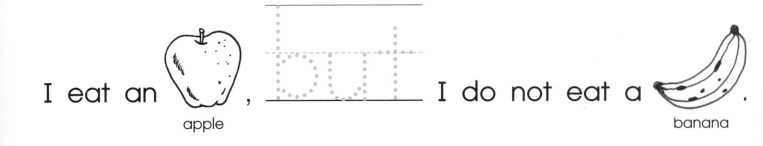

I eat an [apple] , _but_ I do not eat a [banana] .

Name _____

Fishbowl

Draw a line matching the words on the bubbles to the words on the fish.

Yes and No Tic-Tac-Toe

Cut out the words. Take turns placing "yes" and "no" on the game board. The first to get three in a row wins the game.

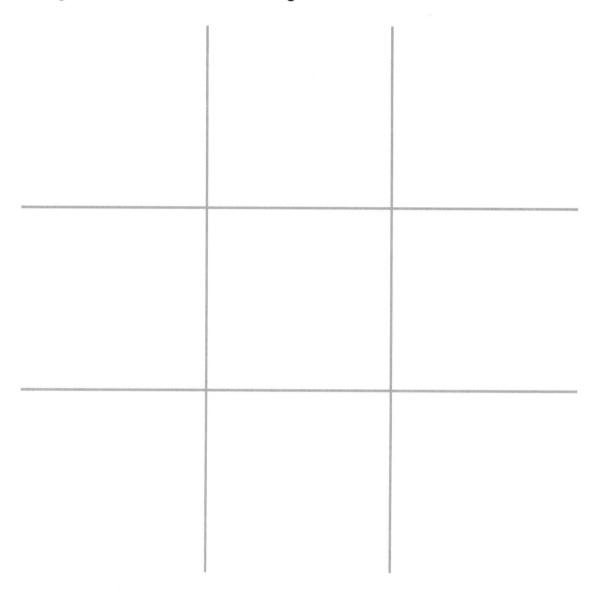

yes	yes	yes	yes	yes
no	no	no	no	no

Snow Days

Cut out the pictures. Glue the things you need for snow under "YES."
Glue the things you do not need in the snow under "NO."

YES	NO

mittens

hat

swimsuit

beach ball

snow boots

flip-flops

Assessment

Circle the word that matches the first word in each row.

and	as	at	and	ant
but	tub	but	be	bat
or	or	on	of	to
so	is	as	son	so
too	to	too	two	so
then	then	than	that	them
as	is	at	as	yes

Listen to your teacher. Draw and label pictures in the boxes.

Overview Question Words

· ·

Directions and Sample Answers for Activity Pages

Day 1	See "Provide a Real-World Example" below.
Day 2	Read aloud the title and directions. Read each question. Encourage students to follow along using the rebus to help them. Read the question twice, using both word choices. Guide students to identify which question word is correct and draw a circle around that word. (who, where, when, why, how)
Day 3	Read aloud the title and directions. Help students read the key and the words in the picture. Model how to use the key to color in each part of the picture. Mystery picture: rainbow.
Day 4	Read aloud the title and directions. Helps students cut, shuffle, and place the words facedown on a table. Show students how to play. Explain that when they make a match, they ask their partner a question using that word. Model an example.
Day 5	Read aloud the title and directions. Allow time for students to complete the first task. Then **ask:** *How do you get to school?* Afterward, meet individually with students to discuss their results. Use their responses to plan further instruction and review.

Provide a Real-World Example

◆ Write the word **why** on chart paper. **Ask:** *Why do we go to school?* Allow responses. Then **say:** *We use the word **why** to ask a question. We use other question words, too.*

◆ Hand out the Day 1 activity page. **Say:** *Let's look at more question words.* Point out the first picture of a face with a question mark. **Ask:** *Who is it? Let's trace **who**.*

◆ Draw attention to the gift. **Ask:** *What is it? Let's trace **what**.* Point out the map and **ask:** *Where is it? Let's trace **where**.* Draw attention to the clock. **Ask:** *When is it? Let's trace **when**.* Now focus on the hands. **Ask:** *Which is it? Let's trace **which**.* Finally, focus on the jar of jelly beans. **Ask:** *How many? Let's trace **how**.*

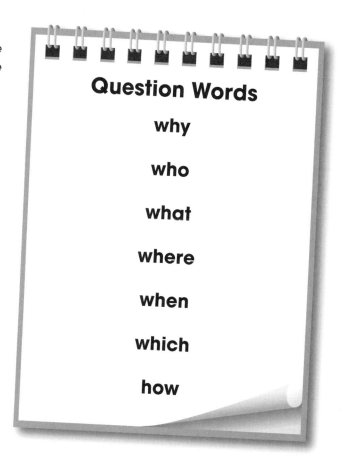

Question Words

why

who

what

where

when

which

how

Questions, Questions

Look at the pictures and question words. Listen to your teacher. Trace each word.

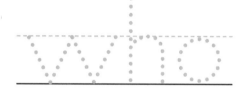

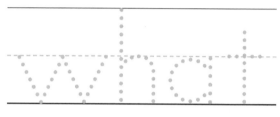

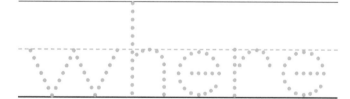

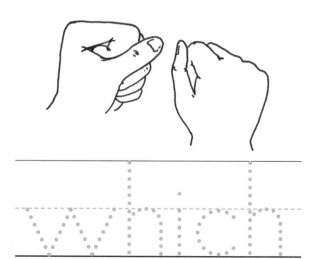

Complete the Question

Circle the word that completes the question.

_____

_____ is the 👦 ?
Why   **Who**   boy

_____

_____ is the 🏠 ?
Where   **Why**   house

_____

_____ is it time to go?
Who   **When**

_____

_____ is the ☀ yellow?
What   **Why**   sun

_____

_____ many ⭐ do you see?
How   **Where**   stars

Name _____

Mystery Picture

Find out the mystery picture. Hint: It sometimes comes after a rain shower.

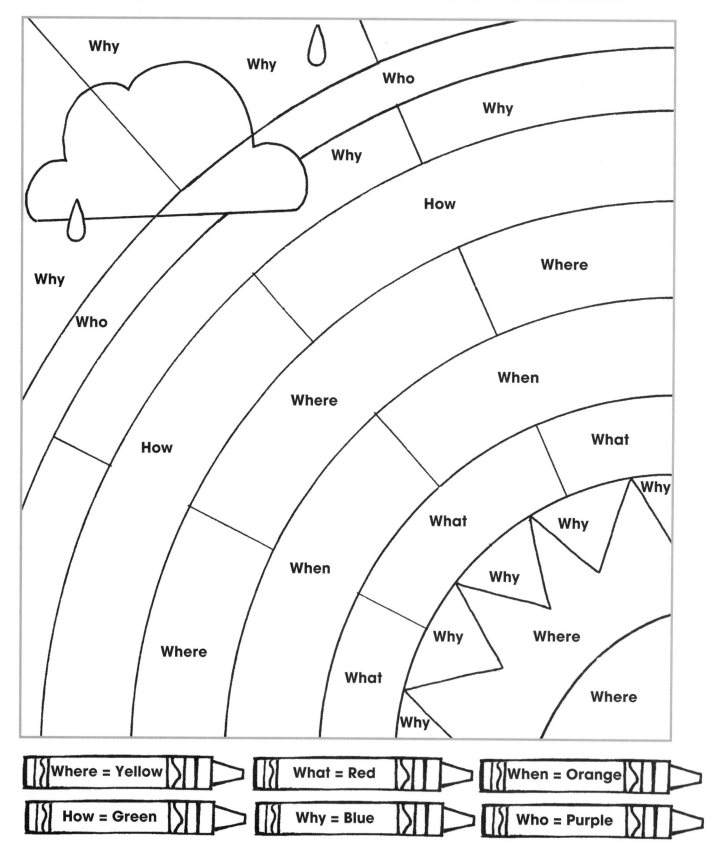

Where = Yellow

What = Red

When = Orange

How = Green

Why = Blue

Who = Purple

Unit 4 • Everyday Vocabulary Intervention Activities Grade K • ©2011 Newmark Learning, LLC

Name _____

Make a Match, Ask a Question

Play with a partner. Cut out the pictures. Turn them over. Take turns trying to make a match. Use your word to ask a question.

who	who	what	what
when	when	where	where
which	which	how	how

Assessment

Draw a line between each picture and a matching question word.

where

which

what

when

who

Listen to your teacher. Draw an answer in the box.

Overview   Nouns: Naming Words

Directions and Sample Answers for Activity Pages

Day 1	See "Provide a Real-World Example" below.
Day 2	Read aloud the title and directions. Help students cut out the pictures and sort them by people, places, and things. Then guide students to glue each group of pictures in a separate square. (People: **mom**, **boy**; Places: **park**, **house**; Things: **toy**, **car**)
Day 3	Read aloud the title and directions. Help students identify the topic of each book. Remind students that Bella likes books about places. Have them find and circle each book about a place. (Bella's books: *The Pond*, *At the Zoo*, *Home Sweet Home*)
Day 4	Read aloud the title and directions. Help students identify each picture as a person, place, or thing, and color as instructed. (Mystery picture: **hat**)
Day 5	Read aloud the title and directions. Allow time for students to complete the first task. Then ask them to draw a person and label the picture. Afterward, meet individually with students to discuss their results. Use their responses to plan further instruction and review.

Provide a Real-World Example

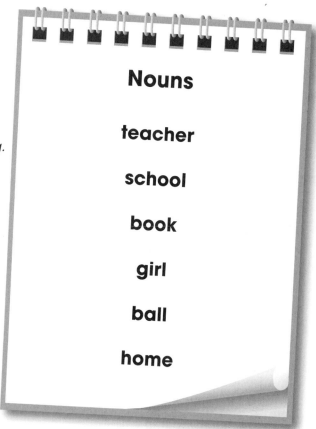

Nouns

teacher

school

book

girl

ball

home

◆ Write **teacher** on the board. **Say:** *I am a teacher. A teacher is a person. Who is a person you know?*

◆ Write **school** on chart paper. **Say:** *School is a place we go to learn. Where are other places you go?*

◆ Point to a book in the classroom. **Say:** *A book is a thing. What are some things you know of or use?* After students answer, **say:** *Teacher, school, and car name people, places, and things. We use these naming words every day.*

◆ Hand out the Day 1 activity page. Point to the girl and **say:** *A girl is a kind of person. Color the girl orange. Trace the word* **girl.** *Point to the ball and* **say:** *A* **ball** *is a thing we play with. Color the ball green. Trace the word* **ball.** *Point to the home and* **say:** *A home is a place where we live. Color the home red. Trace the word* **home.**

People, Places, and Things

Color the girl orange. Color the ball green. Color the home red. Trace the words.

girl

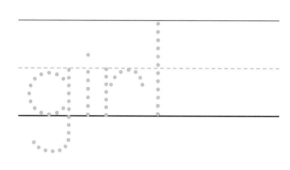

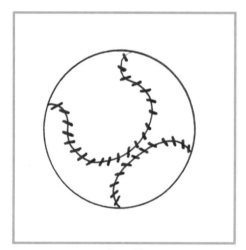

ball

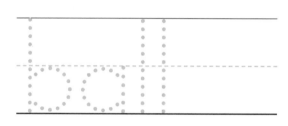

home

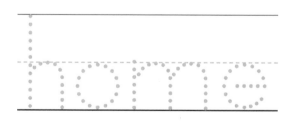

Sort It Out

Cut out the pictures. Glue people in one square. Glue places in one square. Glue things in one square.

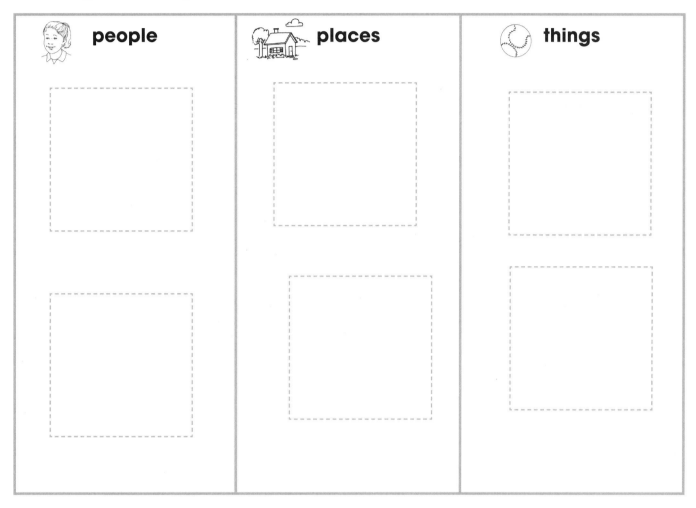

people	places	things

toy	mom	park
boy	car	house

Bella's Books

Bella likes books about places. Circle the books Bella would like.

Unit 5 • Everyday Vocabulary Intervention Activities Grade K • ©2011 Newmark Learning, LLC

Mystery Picture

Find out the mystery picture. Color people red. Color places black. Color things yellow.

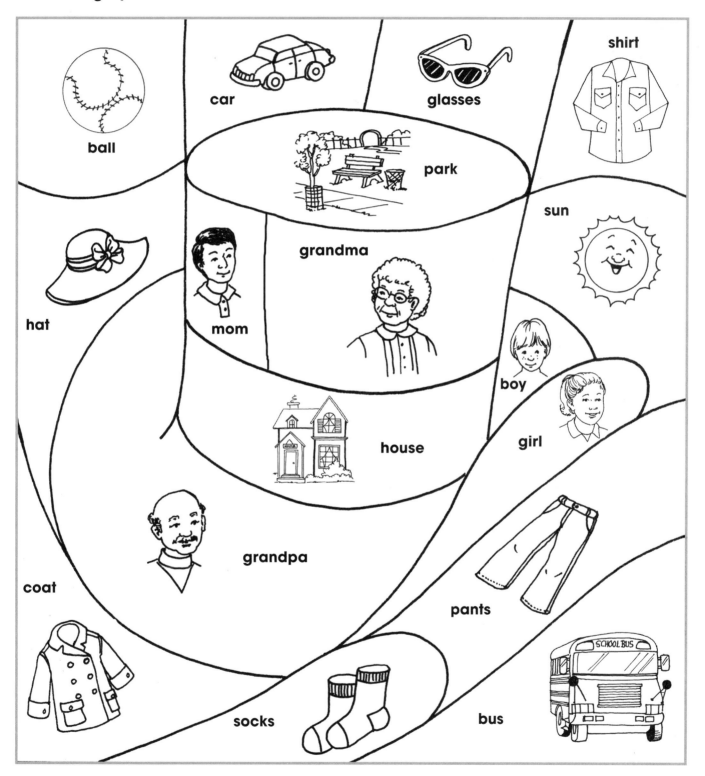

Assessment

Draw a line from each picture to the box labeled "person," "place," or "thing."

person

place

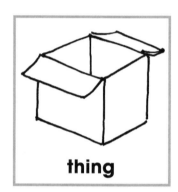

thing

Listen to your teacher. Draw a picture in the box.

Unit 5 • Everyday Vocabulary Intervention Activities Grade K • ©2011 Newmark Learning, LLC

Overview Pronouns and Possessives

Directions and Sample Answers for Activity Pages

Day 1	See "Provide a Real-World Example" below.
Day 2	Read aloud the title and directions. Help students cut out the pictures and glue them on the Bingo card. Explain that when you say **he**, they put an X on one picture of a boy. When you say **she**, they put an X on a girl. And when you say **they**, students are to put an X on a picture with more than one person. Tell them to say "Bingo" when they get three in a row.
Day 3	Read aloud the title and directions. Help students cut out the pictures and identify who owns the item in the picture. Is it a girl/woman, boy/man, or more than one person? Model how to glue a picture in the correct column, and explain why it is in the correct column.
Day 4	Read aloud the title and directions. Guide students to identify which word best completes the sentence and circle it. (I, You, We, They)
Day 5	Read aloud the title and directions. Allow time for students to complete the task. Afterward, meet individually with students to discuss their results. Use their responses to plan further instruction and review.

Provide a Real-World Example

◆ **Say:** *I am a teacher.* Write **I** on chart paper.
Point to a boy and **say:** *He is a student.*
Point to a girl and **say:** *She is a student, too.*
Write **he** and **she** on the chart paper. Now point to your desk and **say:** *This is my desk.* Point to a student's desk and **say:** *This is your desk.* Write **my** and **your** on the chart.

◆ **Say:** *We use the words* **I**, **he**, **she**, **my**, *and* **your** *when we talk, write, and read. We use these words in place of people's names.*

◆ Hand out the Day 1 activity page. **Say:** *Let's look at words that we use in place of people's names.* Draw students' attention to the man. **Say:** *He sleeps.* ***He*** *means the man. Let's trace* ***He****.* Focus on the picture of the skaters. **Say:** *They skate.* ***They*** *means the girl and the boy. Let's trace* ***They****.* Have students look at the hands holding a cup. **Say:** *My cup.* ***My*** *is the word we use to describe the cup that belongs to me.*

◆ Repeat as above with the rest of the pictures and words.

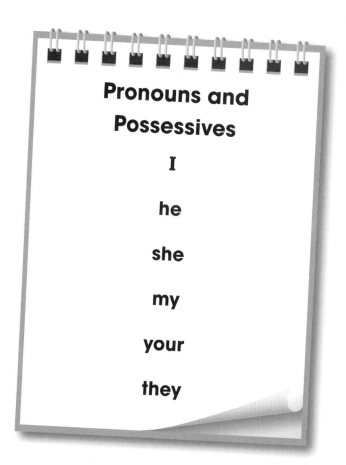

Pronouns and Possessives

I

he

she

my

your

they

People and Their Things

Trace the words.

He sleeps

They skate

My cup

We jump

She cries

Our fire

Their band

He, She, They BINGO

Cut out the pictures. Glue them on the Bingo card. Listen to your teacher. Three in a row is Bingo!

	Free Space	

Hers, His, or Ours?

Cut out the pictures. Glue each picture in the right column.

Make-a-Sentence

Circle the word to complete the sentence.

_____

_____ sleep.

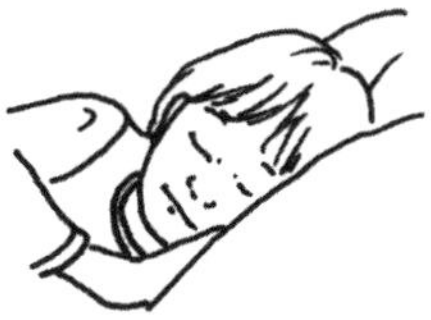

    I   **Me**

_____

_____ run.

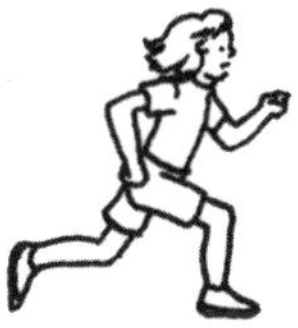

    It   **You**

_____

_____ play.

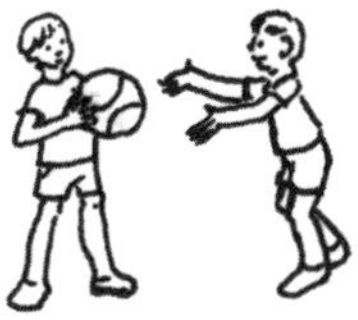

    We   **My**

_____

_____ skate.

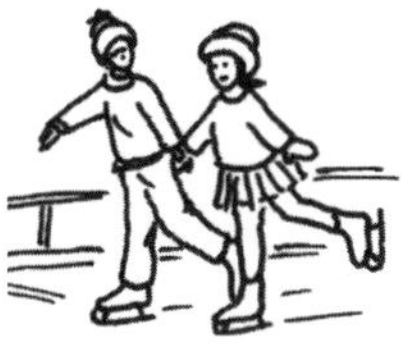

    His   **They**

Assessment

Draw a line between each picture and a matching word.

they

she

he

Overview   Proper Nouns

Directions and Sample Answers for Activity Pages

Day 1	See "Provide a Real-World Example" below.
Day 2	Read aloud the title and directions. Help students cut out the pictures. Discuss what they see in each picture. Point out that the pictures name specific people and places. Help them sort the pictures into people and places and glue them on the page.
Day 3	Read aloud the title and directions. Help students label each member of their family. Remind them to include themselves.
Day 4	Read aloud the title and directions. Help students read the names on the right side. Then guide them to draw a line from each picture to its matching name or names.
Day 5	Read aloud the title and directions. Allow time for students to complete the task. Afterward, meet individually with students to discuss their results. Use their responses to plan further instruction and review.

Provide a Real-World Example

◆ **Ask:** *What is my name? That's right! I am (Mr./Mrs./Ms. your name).* Write your name on chart paper. Now ask a volunteer or two to share their names. Write their names on the chart paper. Then **ask:** *What is the name of our school? That's right! Our school is (name of school). It is in (name of state).*

◆ **Say:** *(Mr./Mrs./Ms. your name), (kids' names from above), and (state) are the names of people and the name of a place. Who are some other people you know? What are some places you visit?* Allow responses. Write their responses on chart paper. **Say:** *We use the names of people and places all the time. When we write them, we use a capital letter at the beginning.*

◆ Hand out the Day 1 activity page. Draw attention to the man, and **say:** *This is Mr. Jones. Let's trace the name **Mr. Jones**. The woman is Mrs. Jones. Let's trace the name **Mrs. Jones**.*

◆ Focus students' attention on the map. **Say:** *Mr. and Mrs. Jones live in New York. Let's trace **New York**. They live on Elm Street. Let's trace **Elm Street**.*

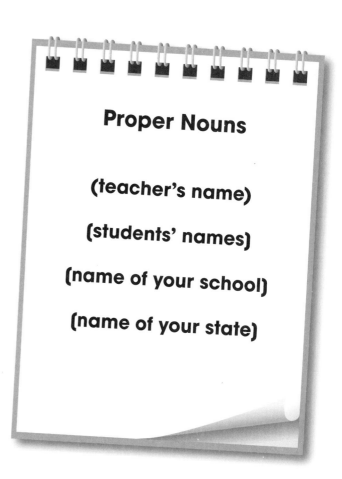

Proper Nouns

(teacher's name)

(students' names)

(name of your school)

(name of your state)

Mr. & Mrs. Jones

Trace each word.

Name _____

Person or Place?

Cut out the pictures. Glue the people on one side. Glue places on the other.

people	places

Officer Smith	Rose Hill School	Munchy Market	Dr. Brown
Mill Avenue	Ms. Glass	Petville Zoo	Jenny

Family Album

Draw a picture of your family. Label each person with his or her name.

Match-Up!

Draw a line from each picture to its matching word or words.

Mr. Hart

Dr. Rose

Jill and Abby

Matt

Assessment

Draw a picture of yourself. Label it.

```
┌──────────────────────────────────────┐
│                                        │
│                                        │
│                                        │
│                                        │
│                                        │              _____
│                                        │
└──────────────────────────────────────┘              _____
```

Draw a picture of your school. Label it.

```
┌──────────────────────────────────────┐
│                                        │
│                                        │
│                                        │
│                                        │
│                                        │              _____
│                                        │
└──────────────────────────────────────┘              _____
```

Draw a picture of your favorite place to go in town. Label it.

```
┌──────────────────────────────────────┐
│                                        │
│                                        │
│                                        │
│                                        │
│                                        │              _____
│                                        │
└──────────────────────────────────────┘              _____
```

Overview   Helping Verbs

Directions and Sample Answers for Activity Pages

Day 1	See "Provide a Real-World Example" below.
Day 2	Read aloud the title and directions. Help students write their name on the first line. Read each sentence and allow time for students to circle their answers. Then ask students to draw a picture of themselves in the box.
Day 3	Read aloud the title and directions. Read each sentence and help students find the picture to match. Guide them to draw a line from the sentence to the picture.
Day 4	Read aloud the title and directions. Read each question. Help students identify and circle the correct answers.
Day 5	Read aloud the title and directions. Read aloud the first prompt. Allow time for students to draw the picture. Repeat with the second prompt. Afterward, meet individually with students to discuss their results. Use their responses to plan further instruction and review.

Provide a Real-World Example

◆ **Say:** *I am a teacher.* Write **am** on chart paper. Then **say:** *You are students.* Write **are** on the chart paper. **Say:** *This is our classroom.* Write **is** on the chart paper.

◆ **Say:** ***Am***, ***are***, and ***is*** *are words that we use every day. These special words help make sense of what we say, read, and write. Listen to how this sentence would sound without the word* ***am***: *I a teacher. Now listen to the sentence with the word* ***am***: *I am a teacher. The word* ***am*** *helps the sentence make sense. This week we will explore other words that help us.*

◆ Hand out the Day 1 activity page. Read the first sentence. **Say:** *The word* ***is*** *helps this sentence make sense. Let's trace the word* ***is***. *Now read the next sentence.* **Say:** *The word* ***has*** *tells us about the boy. Without* ***has***, *the sentence would not make sense. Listen: The boy a kite. Let's trace the word* ***has***. Continue with the remaining sentences.

Helping Verbs

am

are

is

has

Trace-a-Word

Listen to your teacher. Trace each word.

She is a girl.

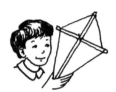

He has a kite.

I can jump.

You are running.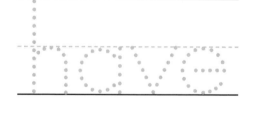

We have books.

He does wear glasses.

All About Me

Write your name. Then circle one answer in each sentence.

My name is _____ .

I am a      .

        boy    girl

I am   .

    four    five    six

I have   .

   long hair    short hair

This is what I look like:

Match-Up!

Draw a line to match the words and pictures.

It is round.

I am sad.

They are happy.

We do run.

It has wheels.

She can swim.

Name _____

Answers, Please!

Listen to your teacher read the question. Circle an answer.

Who is tall?

Which has wheels?

Which can hop?

Which are hot?

Name _____

Assessment

Listen to your teacher. Draw a picture to complete each sentence.

I have . . .

I can . . .

Overview   Action Verbs

Directions and Sample Answers for Activity Pages

Day 1	See "Provide a Real-World Example" below.
Day 2	Read aloud the title and directions. Divide the class into pairs. Help pairs cut out pictures, mix them up, and lay them out facedown. Show how to play by turning over two cards. Tell students they will keep the cards if they make a match. If they do not make a match, they return the cards to their spots facedown.
Day 3	Read aloud the title and directions. Read each sentence twice, using a different answer choice. Ask students which action word sounds right. Guide them to circle the correct word and write it on the line.
Day 4	Read aloud the title and directions. With students, read the word on each lily pad. Help them identify the word as an action or not. Guide them to color the lily pads with action words.
Day 5	Read aloud the title and directions. Read aloud the first prompt. Allow time for students to draw the picture. Read aloud the next prompt, and again allow time to draw. Repeat with the third prompt. Afterward, meet individually with students to discuss their results. Use their responses to plan further instruction and review.

Provide a Real-World Example

Action Words

run

come

eats

slides

rides

says

◆ Run into the classroom. Write **run** on chart paper as you say the word **run**. Then **say:** *I can run! Running is something we do. It is an action. So* **run** *is an action word.*

◆ Invite a student to come toward you. Write **come** on the chart paper and **say:** ***Come*** *is an action word, too. It tells about your classmate's action.*

◆ Invite students to think of other action words. Add their words to the list on the chart paper.

◆ Hand out the Day 1 activity page. **Say:** *A fun park is full of action words. The boy eats ice cream.* ***Eats*** *is an action word. Trace the word* **eats**. *Draw attention to the girl in the inner tube.* **Say:** *The girl slides down.* ***Slides*** *is an action word. Trace the word* **slides**. *Now focus on the girl in the bumper car.* **Say:** *She rides in a car.* ***Rides*** *is an action word, too. Trace the word* **rides**. *Now point out the boy on the ride with his arms in the air.* **Say:** *The boy is scared! He says, "Help!"* ***Says*** *is an action word. Trace the word* **says**.

Name _____

The Fun Park

Look at the pictures. Listen to your teacher. Trace the action words.

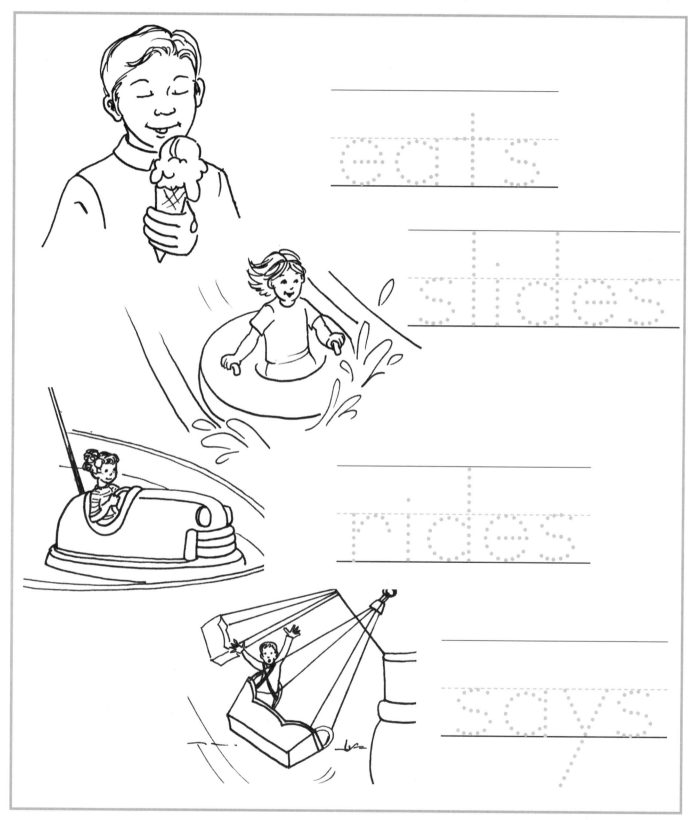

eats

slides

rides

says

Action Word Make-a-Match

**Play with a partner. Cut out the pictures. Turn them over.
Take turns trying to make a match.**

look

eat

play

run

ride

Circle It. Write It.

Listen to your teacher. Circle the correct word for each sentence. Write it on the line.

I _____   home .

    come   **comes**

He _____   home .

    come   **comes**

She _____ to   school .

    go   **goes**

I _____ to   school .

    go   **goes**

She _____ a   rainbow .

    see   **sees**

I _____ a   rainbow .

    see   **sees**

Unit 9 • Everyday Vocabulary Intervention Activities Grade K • ©2011 Newmark Learning, LLC

Leap Frog

Get Froggy across the pond. Color the lily pads with action words.

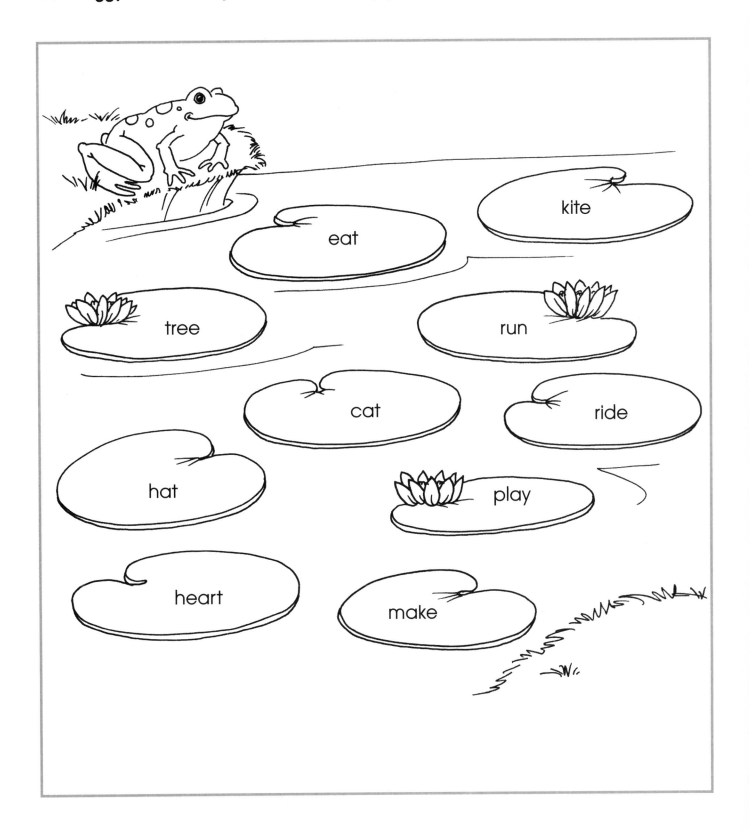

Assessment

Listen to your teacher. Draw a picture to complete each sentence.

I like to . . .

I see a . . .

I make a . . .

Overview   Adjectives: Describing Words

Directions and Sample Answers for Activity Pages

Day 1	See "Provide a Real-World Example" below.
Day 2	Read aloud the title and directions. Help students cut out the pictures. For each picture, ask if it is something they would use or do on a snowy day or a sunny day. Then guide them to glue the picture under the snow or the sun. (Snowy: **boots**, **coat**, **snowman**; Sunny: **glasses**, **shorts**, **swim**)
Day 3	Read aloud the title and directions. Tell students to look at each picture and decide if it is something that is big or little. Then help draw a line connecting the path of little things. (Little path: **ant**, **acorn**, **worm**, **leaf**, **flower**, **bee**)
Day 4	Read aloud the title and directions. **Say:** Draw something that makes you mad. When students complete the drawing, **say:** Draw something that makes you glad.
Day 5	Read aloud the title and directions. Read aloud the word in each row. Tell students to draw a circle around the picture that shows that word. Allow time between words. After students complete the first task, ask them to draw something that makes them feel happy. Afterward, meet individually with students to discuss their results. Use their responses to plan further instruction and review.

Provide a Real-World Example

◆ Invite some students to the front of the classroom to stand next to you. Point to yourself and **say:** *I am big.* Point to the students and **say:** *Kids are little.* Write **big** and **little** on chart paper. **Say: *Big*** *and* ***little*** *are words that tell about size.*

◆ Direct students' attention to the weather. **Ask:** *What is the weather like today?* Write their responses on the chart paper. **Say:** *We use words like* **sunny**, **cloudy**, *and* **rainy** *to tell about the weather. These words help us picture what the weather is like.*

◆ Hand out the Day 1 activity page. Invite students to focus on the first picture. **Ask:** *How does the girl feel?* Allow responses. Then **say:** *Yes, the girl is happy.* ***Happy*** *is a word we use to tell how someone feels. Let's trace the word* **happy**. Now focus on the next picture. **Say:** *The dog is big. The cat is little.* ***Big*** *and* ***little*** *tell about the pets' sizes. Let's trace* **big** *and* **little**. Now draw attention to the rain. **Say:** *The weather is rainy in this picture.* ***Rainy*** *is a word we use to tell about the weather. Let's trace* **rainy**.

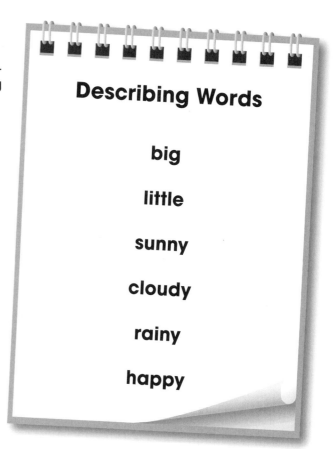

Describing Words

big

little

sunny

cloudy

rainy

happy

Name _____

Describe and Trace

Listen to your teacher. Trace the words.

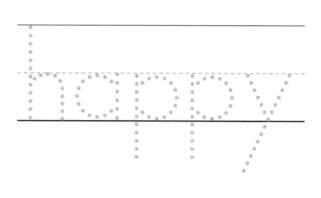

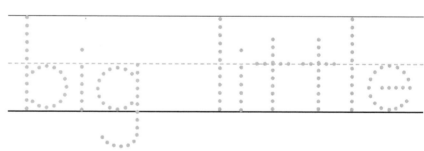

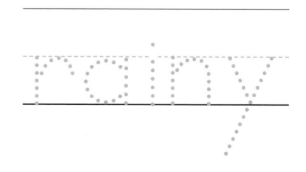

Name _____

Snowy or Sunny?

Cut out the pictures. Glue each under the correct picture.

Snowy	Sunny

coat	boots	shorts
snowman	**glasses**	**swim**

Mouse House

Help Mouse find his house. Connect the path of little things.

Mad Me. Glad Me.

**Listen to your teacher. Draw a picture of something that makes you mad.
Draw a picture of something that makes you glad.**

Mad	**Glad**

Assessment

Listen to your teacher. Circle the picture that shows what the word means.

happy			
sad			
mad			
big			
cloudy			
sunny			

Listen to your teacher. Draw your picture.

Overview Synonyms and Antonyms

Directions and Sample Answers for Activity Pages

Day 1	See "Provide a Real-World Example" below.
Day 2	Read aloud the title and directions. Remind students what **opposite** means by giving an example, such as big and small. Help students to identify each picture and guide them to draw the opposite. As an extra challenge, invite students to label their pictures.
Day 3	Read aloud the title and directions. Help students read the words in one column. Then help them identify words that mean the same thing in the other column. Model how to draw a line between the words that mean the same thing.
Day 4	Read aloud the title and directions. Divide the class into pairs. Help pairs cut out pictures, mix them up, and lay them facedown. Show how to play by turning over two cards. Tell students they keep the cards if they find opposites. If they do not, they return the cards to their spots facedown.
Day 5	Read aloud the title and directions. Allow time for students to complete the task. Afterward, meet individually with students to discuss their results. Use their responses to plan further instruction and review.

Provide a Real-World Example

◆ Stomp your feet and make an angry face. **Ask:** *How do I feel?* (Allow responses.) *Yes, I feel angry. Another word for how I feel is* **mad**. **Angry** *and* **mad** *mean the same thing.* Write **angry** and **mad** on chart paper.

◆ Show a paper clip to the class. Then point to the desk. **Say:** *Which is big? Which is little?* (Allow responses.) **Say:** *Yes, the paper clip is little and the desk is big.* **Big** *and* **little** *mean different things. They are opposites.* Write **big** and **little** on the chart paper. **Ask:** *What are some other opposites you know?* Add them to the list on the chart.

◆ Hand out the Day 1 activity page. Read aloud each pair of words, and ask if they mean the same thing or not. For example, **ask:** *Do* **little** *and* **small** *mean the same thing or are they opposites?* (Allow responses.) **Little** *and* **small** *mean the same, so let's check the "Same" column.*

Same-Meaning Words

angry/mad

Opposite-Meaning Words

big/little

Check It!

Listen to your teacher read the words. Check "Same" or "Opposite."

				Same	**Opposite**
little		small		☐	☐
big		large		☐	☐
big		little		☐	☐
glad		mad		☐	☐
happy		glad		☐	☐
sad		happy		☐	☐
rainy		sunny		☐	☐
more		less		☐	☐

Opposite Pictures

Look at each picture. Draw a picture that shows the opposite.

big 	
sad 	
sunny 	
happy 	

Match-Up!

Draw a line to match pictures that mean the same thing.

happy

large

mad

glad

big

little

small

angry

Memory Game

Cut out the pictures. Lay them facedown. Match opposite pictures.

| happy | sad | big | small |
| sunny | rainy | more | less |

Assessment

Listen to your teacher read each pair of words. If they mean the same, color the heart red. If they do not mean the same, color the heart blue.

little	small	♡
big	small	♡
happy	glad	♡
more	less	♡
happy	sad	♡
big	large	♡
rainy	sunny	♡

Overview   Multiple-Meaning Words

Directions and Sample Answers for Activity Pages

Day 1	See "Provide a Real-World Example" below.
Day 2	Read aloud the title and directions. **Say:** *Saw means two things. One **saw** is a tool to cut wood. A saw is very sharp. The other **saw** means to have seen something.* Read aloud each sentence. Help students identify which meaning of **saw** is used in each sentence. Guide them to draw a circle around the correct word.
Day 3	Tell students that the word **like** means two things. **Say:** *The girl is like her mom. They both have red hair.* Then **say:** *I like ice cream.* Point out that the first example means how two things are the same and the second means "enjoy." Read aloud the title and the first prompt. Allow time for students to draw the first picture. Then read the second prompt and allow time to draw the second picture.
Day 4	Read aloud the title and directions. Explain that the word **ride** is an action word (or verb). You can ride a bike. A ride can also be a thing (or a noun) such as a roller coaster at an amusement park. The first ride is something you do, or an action. The second is a thing that you can go on. Help students color each noun **ride** in blue. Help students color each verb **ride** yellow.
Day 5	**Say:** *Can. I eat a can of soup.* Tell students to draw a picture that shows the word **can**. Then **say:** *Like. I like flowers.* Tell students to draw a picture that shows **like**. **Say:** *Ride. I ride a horse.* Tell students to draw a picture that shows **ride**. Afterward, meet individually with students to discuss their results. Use their responses to plan further instruction and review.

Provide a Real-World Example

◆ Hold up a can and **say:** *I put things inside a can.* Write **can** on chart paper and repeat the word. Put pencils in the can as you **say:** *I can put pencils inside.* Repeat the word **can** as you point to it on the chart paper.

◆ **Say:** ***Can** means two things.* Hold up the can and **say:** *This **can** is a thing I can use. The other **can** means being able to do something. We use words that have more than one meaning all the time. We can figure out what meaning a word has by thinking about how it is used in a sentence.*

◆ Hand out the Day 1 activity page. **Say:** *Listen to me read each sentence. Let's draw a circle around the word **can** when it means something that we put things in. Let's draw a line under the word **can** when it means being able to do something.* Read the first sentence. Then **say:** *This **can** is the kind we put things in. Let's draw a circle around it.*

◆ Read aloud the next sentence. **Say:** *This **can** means I am able to swim. Let's draw a line under it.* Read the next sentence. **Ask:** *What does this **can** mean?* (Allow responses.) Then **say:** *Yes, this **can** means I am able to see you. Let's draw a line under it.* Continue with the rest of the sentences.

Multiple-Meaning Words

can

saw

like

ride

Can Can

Listen to your teacher. Draw a circle around the word "can" when it means something we use to put things in. Draw a line under the word "can" when it means "able to."

I put water in the can.

I can swim.

I can see you.

I ate a can of soup.

Can you sing?

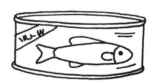

I ate a can of tuna fish.

Complete the Sentence

Listen to your teacher. Draw a circle around the tool or the eye
to show which answer is the right one.

He used a saw to
cut down the tree.

saw

saw

I saw birds.

saw

saw

Do not touch
the saw.

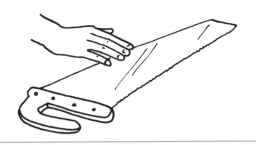

saw

saw

We saw a play.

saw

saw

Like and Like

Think of a friend you are most like. Draw a picture to show how you are the same.

What do you like to eat? Draw a picture.

Ride! Ride! Ride!

Color things you ride blue. Color the action of riding yellow.

Assessment

Listen to your teacher say each word and use the word in a sentence.
Draw a picture of the word.

can

like

ride

Overview Everyday Content Words

Directions and Sample Answers for Activity Pages

Day 1	See "Provide a Real-World Example" below.
Day 2	Read aloud the title and directions. Help students draw the people in their family. Then help them cut out the words and read each one together. If their picture includes that person, help them glue the word next to that person.
Day 3	Read aloud the title and directions. Help students identify the pictures on the dog bones as you read aloud each one. Then guide students to color the bones with pets.
Day 4	Read aloud the title and directions. Help pairs of students cut out one set of pictures and fold them. Model how to play charades. Choose one of the folded pictures. Act out the person or pet. Encourage students to guess who or what you are.
Day 5	Read aloud the title and directions. Allow time for students to complete the task. Afterward, meet individually with students to discuss their results. Use their responses to plan further instruction and review.

Provide a Real-World Example

◆ **Ask:** *Who is in your family?* Allow a couple of volunteers to answer. Write their responses on chart paper. Read aloud the list as you point to each family member name.

◆ **Ask:** *Who has a pet? What kind of pet do you have?* Allow responses. Then write responses on chart paper and read aloud.

◆ **Say:** *This week we will focus on words for people in our families and our pets.*

◆ Hand out the Day 1 activity page. **Say:** *This is a family. Who is in this family?* Direct students' attention to the father. **Say:** *This is the dad. Color in the dad. Trace the word **dad**.* **Ask:** *Which person is the mom?* (Allow responses.) *Right! The woman is the mom. Let's color in the mom. Now trace the word **mom**.* Repeat these steps with **brother**, **sister**, and **cat**.

Everyday Content Words

dad

mom

brother

sister

cat

My Family

Color each person and pet in the family. Trace each word.

dad

mom

brother

sister

cat

Family Photo

Draw a picture of your family. Cut out the words. Glue each word next to the person.

mom	**dad**	**sister**	**brother**
cat	**dog**	**fish**	**bird**

Name _____

Go Home, Spot!

Help Spot go home. Color the trail of bones that have pets on them.

Unit 13 • Everyday Vocabulary Intervention Activities Grade K • ©2011 Newmark Learning, LLC

Charades

Cut out the pictures. Fold them up. Pick a picture. Do not show your partner.
Act out the person or pet for your partner to guess.

dad	mom	brother	sister
dog	cat	fish	bird

Assessment

Cut out the pictures. Glue the people on one side. Glue the pets on the other side.

People	Pets

dad	mom	brother	sister

dog	cat	fish	bird

Overview   Everyday Concept Words

Directions and Sample Answers for Activity Pages

Day 1	See "Provide a Real-World Example" below.
Day 2	Read aloud the title and directions. Guide students to look at each row. Help them identify which item is different from the others. Help them notice that three words are alike and one is different. Tell them to put an X on the picture/word that is different.
Day 3	Read aloud the title and directions. Helps students identify the pictures around the center. If a picture shows a food, guide them to draw a line from the food to the center picture.
Day 4	Prepare by writing the following eight words on scraps of paper and putting them in a container: **ball, coat, eat, pants, play, socks, shirt, hat**. Help students cut out the pictures and glue them on the Bingo card. Pick a word from the container. Read it aloud and write it on the board. Guide students to find the word on their Bingo card, and put an X on the word. Tell them they have "Bingo" when they get three in a row.
Day 5	**Say:** *I like tennis. What do you like? Draw a picture in the first box.* Allow students time to draw. Then **say:** *I eat an apple. What do you like to eat? Draw a picture in the second box.* Allow time for students to draw. Then **say:** *I have a cup. What do you have? Draw a picture in the third box.* Allow time for students to complete the third picture. Afterward, meet individually with students to discuss their results. Use their responses to plan further instruction and review.

Provide a Real-World Example

◆ **Say:** *I like to teach. I also like to play tennis.* Write **like** and **play** on chart paper. **Ask:** *What do you like to do? What do you like to play?* Allow responses.

◆ **Say:** *I have a tennis racket. I use my racket to play tennis.* Write **have** on the list. **Ask:** *What do you have?*

◆ **Say:** *Like*, *play*, and *have* are words we use every day. This week we will focus on everyday words like these.

◆ Hand out the Day 1 activity page. Direct attention to the first picture. Read the sentence. Repeat the word **like**. **Say:** *Let's trace the word **like**.* Read the second sentence. Repeat the word **eat**. **Say:** *Let's trace the word **eat**.* Continue reading sentences and tracing words.

Everyday Concept Words

like

play

have

eat

shirt

hat

ball

Trace-a-Word

Trace each word.

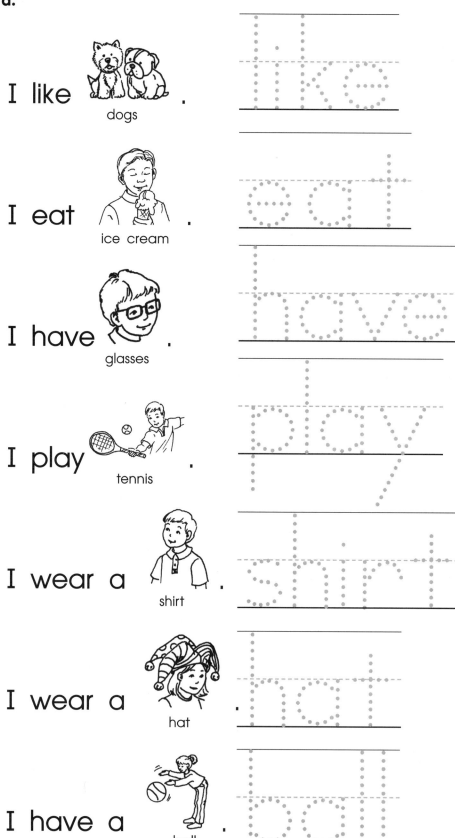

I like 🐕 .
dogs

I eat 🍦 .
ice cream

I have 👓 .
glasses

I play 🎾 .
tennis

I wear a 👕 .
shirt

I wear a 🎭 .
hat

I have a ⚽ .
ball

Name _____

Which Is Different?

Look at the pictures. Draw an X on the one that is not like the others.

sock	shirt	sock	sock
ball	ball	ball	hat
pants	shoe	shoe	shoe
hat	hat	coat	hat

Eat Up!

Draw a line from the center to things we eat.

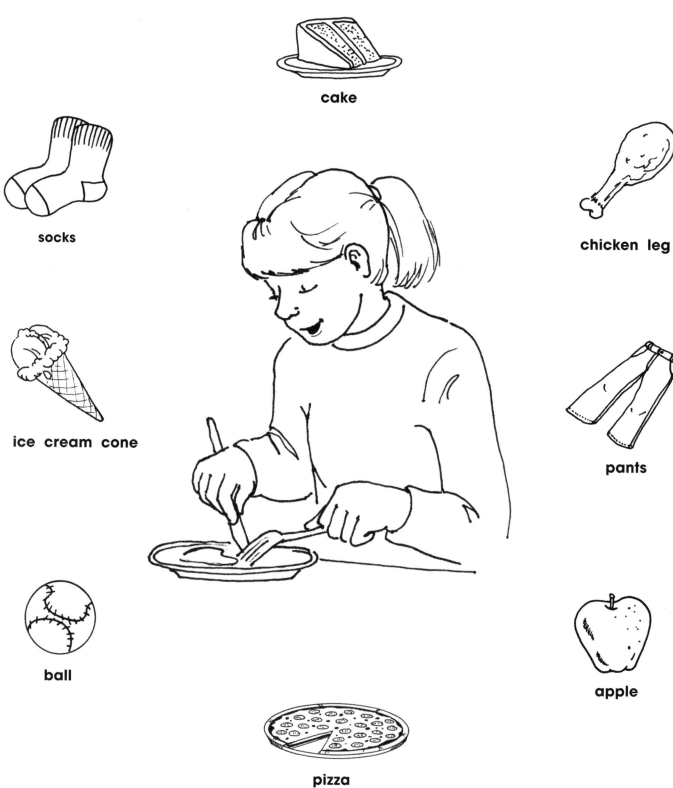

cake

socks

chicken leg

ice cream cone

pants

ball

apple

pizza

Name _____

Bingo!

Cut out the pictures. Glue them into the squares on the Bingo card. Listen to the words your teacher calls out. Put an X on the word. Three in a row wins Bingo!

	Free Space	

ball	coat	eat	pants
play	**socks**	**shirt**	**hat**

Assessment

Listen to your teacher. Draw the pictures.

I like . . .

I eat . . .

I have . . .

Overview Social Studies Words: Geography and Citizenship

- -

Directions and Sample Answers for Activity Page

Day 1	See "Provide a Real-World Example" below.
Day 2	Read aloud the title and directions. Explain that the map shows a walk through town. Point out the numbers on the map and the ones before the sentences. Help students cut out the pictures. Read each sentence starter, and guide students to glue in the right picture.
Day 3	Read aloud the title and directions. **Say:** *We eat and do many things at parties and other celebrations.* Review the words **eat** and **do**. Help students cut out the pictures and identify each as something they eat or do. Help students glue each picture under **eat** or **do**.
Day 4	Read aloud the title and directions. Help students draw the flag. Then read aloud each sentence starter and possible answers. Guide students to draw a circle around the correct answer. For the third sentence, help students by counting the colors in the flag in your classroom.
Day 5	Read aloud the title and directions. Read aloud each prompt, allowing time between for students to draw their answers. **Say:** *At parties, I eat . . .* Then **say:** *My flag has . . .* Invite students to draw something the flag has on it. Finally **say:** *A map of my town has . . .* Invite students to draw a place they'd see on a map of their town. Afterward, meet individually with students to discuss their results. Use their responses to plan further instruction and review.

Provide a Real-World Example

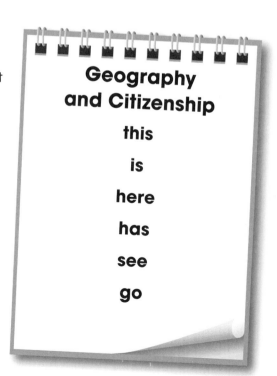

♦ Display a map. It may be a state map, a U.S. map, or a world map. **Say:** *This is a map.* Write **this** and **is** on chart paper. Point to your town, state, or country on the map and **say:** *We are here.* Write **here** on the chart paper. Then **say:** *A map has many things. It has towns, states, or countries. It has bodies of water, forests, parks, schools, and more.* Write **has** on the chart paper.

♦ **Ask:** *What do you see on this map?* Write **see** on the chart paper. (Allow responses.)

♦ Hand out the Day 1 activity page. **Say:** *This is a map of a town. The map has many places on it.* Focus attention on the school. **Say:** *The children go to school. Let's color the school. Let's trace the word go.* Now direct attention on the park. **Say:** *Here is a park. Let's color the park. Let's trace the word here.* Point out the library. **Say:** *I see a library. Let's color the library. Let's trace the word see.* Ask students to find the houses. **Say:** *The town has many houses. Let's color the houses. Let's trace the word has.*

Geography
and Citizenship
this
is
here
has
see
go

Town Map

Listen to your teacher. Color the places. Trace the words.

The children __go__ to school.

__Here__ is a park.

I __see__ a library.

The town __has__ many houses.

Maps

Cut out the pictures. Look at the route on the map. Listen to your teacher read the sentence starters. Glue the pictures to complete each sentence.

1. I start at my

2. Then I go to the

3. Next, I go to the

4. After, I go to the

5. Finally, I go to the

park

bakery

market

house

ice cream shop

Celebrate!

Cut out the pictures. Glue things you eat at a party on one side.
Glue things you do at a party on the other.

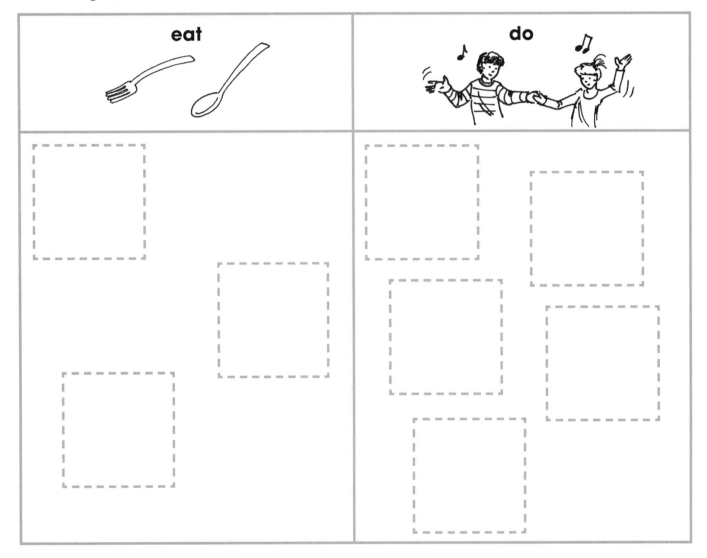

Our Flag

Draw and color in your country's flag. Then circle answers to complete each sentence.

My 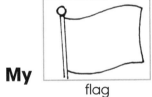 **has**    .

flag   flowers   stars   hearts

My 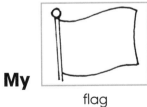 **has** 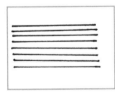   .

flag   stripes   trees   fish

My 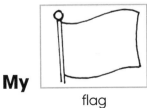 **has**  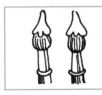 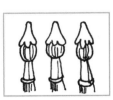 .

flag   1 color   2 colors   3 colors

Assessment

Listen to your teacher. Draw a picture to complete each sentence.

At parties, I eat . . .

My flag has . . .

A map of my town has . . .

Overview Social Studies Words: Jobs and Transportation

Directions and Sample Answers for Activity Pages

Day 1	See "Provide a Real-World Example" below.
Day 2	Read aloud the title and directions. Help students cut out and identify each type of transportation. Help them read the labels and match the pictures to the labels. Then guide them to glue each picture in its box.
Day 3	Read aloud the title and directions. Read aloud each sentence. Help students identify the two answer choices. Guide them to draw a circle around the picture that shows what each worker would have.
Day 4	Read aloud the title and directions. Help students identify the workers and the kinds of transportation they ride in. Then guide them to make matches by drawing a line between the two.
Day 5	Read aloud the title and directions. **Say:** *I can . . .* and invite students to draw something they can do. Allow time for students to draw. Then say: *I go to . . .* Invite students to draw somewhere they go. After they draw, **say:** *I ride in a . . .* Invite students to draw a form of transportation they ride in. Afterward, meet individually with students to discuss their results. Use their responses to plan further instruction and review.

Provide a Real-World Example

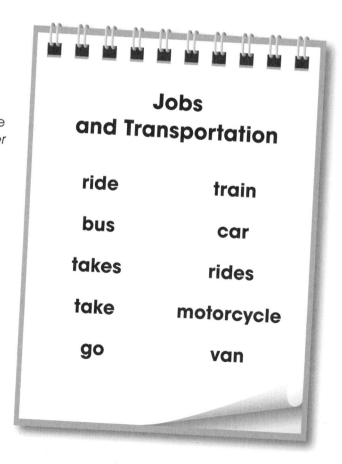

Jobs and Transportation

ride   train

bus   car

takes   rides

take   motorcycle

go   van

◆ Point to a school bus outside, or show a picture of one. **Say:** *Many children ride in a bus like this one. A bus driver takes children to school.* Write **ride**, **bus**, and **takes** on chart paper. **Ask:** *How do your parents go to work?* Write students' responses on the chart paper. **Say:** *Some parents go on a train. Other parents take a bus. Still others go in a car.* Write **take**, **go**, **train**, and **car** on the chart paper.

◆ **Say:** *There are many ways to get around our town. There are many different kinds of workers, like a bus driver, in our town, too. This week we will explore words about transportation and workers.*

◆ Hand out the Day 1 activity page. Focus attention on the first picture. **Say:** *The firefighter rides a truck. Trace the word **rides**.* Now look at the second picture. **Say:** *The bus driver rides a bus. Trace the word **rides**.* Look at the third picture. **Say:** *The police officer rides a motorcycle. Trace the word **rides**.* Look at the last picture. **Say:** *The painter rides a van. Trace the word **rides**.* Now **ask:** *How do you ride to school? Draw a picture.*

Getting Around Town

Listen to your teacher. Trace the words.

The
firefighter
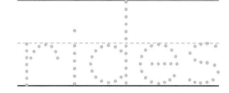 a  .
firetruck

The
bus driver
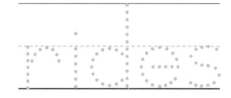 a 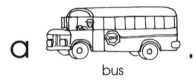 .
bus

The
police officer
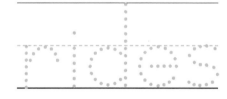 a  .
motorcycle

The
painter
 a  .
van

Beep! Beep!

Cut out the pictures. Glue them in the correct boxes.

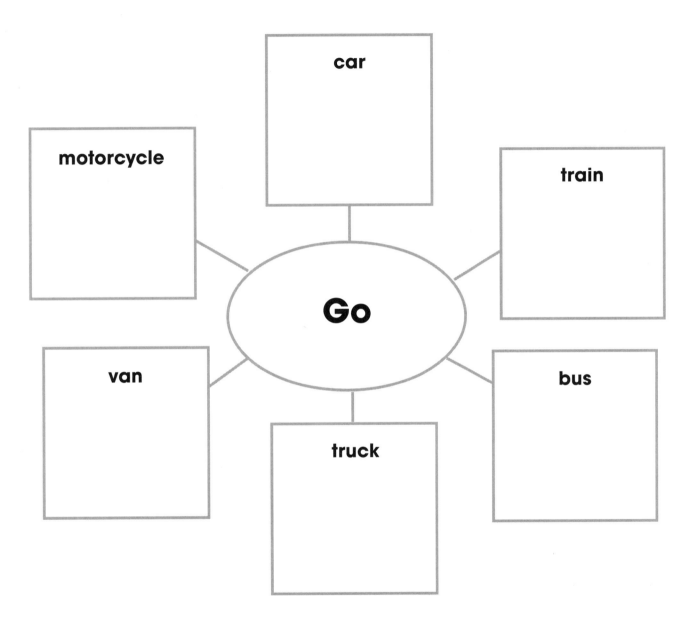

What Do You Have?

Listen to your teacher. Circle the picture that best finishes each sentence.

A  firefighter has a  hose 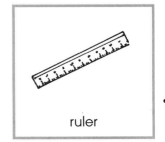 ruler .

A  mail carrier has a 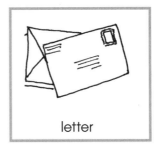 letter  stethoscope .

A  teacher has a  spoon  ruler .

A  doctor has a  stethoscope 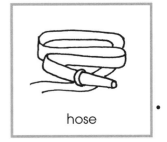 hose .

A  bus driver has a  bus 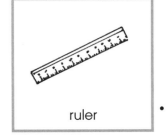 ruler .

Transportation and Jobs

Draw a line to match the worker with his or her transportation.

bus driver

 **motorcycle**

firefighter

 **train**

police officer

 **bus**

painter

 **van**

conductor

 **truck**

Assessment

Listen to your teacher. Draw a picture to complete each sentence.

I can . . .

I go to . . .

I ride in a . . .

Overview   Science Words: Animal Habitats

Directions and Sample Answers for Activity Pages

Day 1	See "Provide a Real-World Example" below.
Day 2	Read aloud the title and directions. Help students identify each picture and read the label aloud. Show students how to color the animals brown and the plants green.
Day 3	Read aloud the title and directions. Read aloud each sentence, including the two answer choices. Help students figure out which answer is correct and draw a circle around the answer. Then read the second task. Guide students to draw an animal that lives in the desert.
Day 4	Prepare for the game by writing the following words on scraps of paper and putting them in a container: **tree**, **plant**, **fish**, **sand**, **hot**, **cold**, **wet**, **dry**. Help students cut out the words and glue them on the Bingo card. Pick a word, write it on the board, and read it aloud. Tell student to find that word and put an X on it. Tell them to say "Bingo" when they get three in a row.
Day 5	Read aloud the title and directions. Allow time for students to complete the first task. Then **say:** An ocean has . . . and direct students to draw a plant or animal that lives in an ocean. Afterward, meet individually with students to discuss their results. Use their responses to plan further instruction and review.

Provide a Real-World Example

◆ Show pictures of plants and animals from a habitat, such as a pond. Then ask students where they might see these living things. For example, **say:** *Frog, fish, grass, and lily pad. Where do these animals and plants live?* (Allow responses.) **Say:** *Yes! These plants and animals live in a pond.* Write **plants** and **animals** on the chart paper.

◆ **Say:** *A pond is a kind of habitat, or place where natural things live. Different habitats have different weather, plants, and animals. This week we will explore habitat words.*

◆ Hand out the Day 1 activity page. **Say:** *Welcome to the rain forest! Many plants and animals live here. Can you find all of them?* Point to the snake. **Say:** *A snake is an animal. Let's trace the word* **animal**. *Let's color the snake.* Now point to a tree. **Say:** *A tree is a plant. Let's trace the word* **plant**. *Let's color the tree.* Repeat as above with each animal and plant.

Welcome to the Rain Forest

Color each plant and animal. Trace the words "plant" and "animal."

Name _____

Animal or Plant?

Color the animals brown. Color the plants green.

All About the Desert

Listen to your teacher. Circle the word that best completes each sentence.

desert

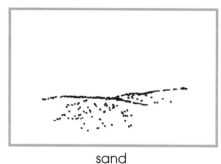

sand

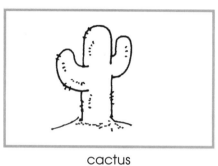

cactus

This desert is | **hot** | **cold** | .

This desert is | **wet** | **dry** | .

This desert | **has** | **have** | sand.

What else does a desert have? Draw an animal that lives in the desert.

Habitat Bingo

Cut out the pictures. Glue them into the squares on the Bingo card.
Listen to your teacher. Put an X on the correct picture. Three in a row wins Bingo!

	Free Space	

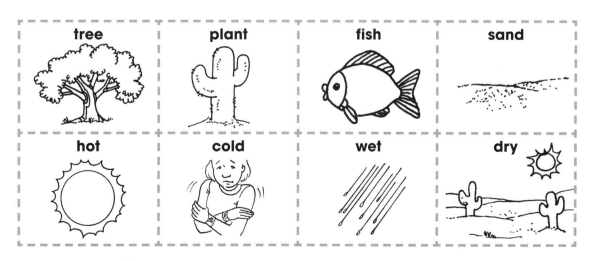

| tree | plant | fish | sand |
| hot | cold | wet | dry |

Assessment

Cut out the pictures. Glue animals on the animal side. Glue plants on the plant side.

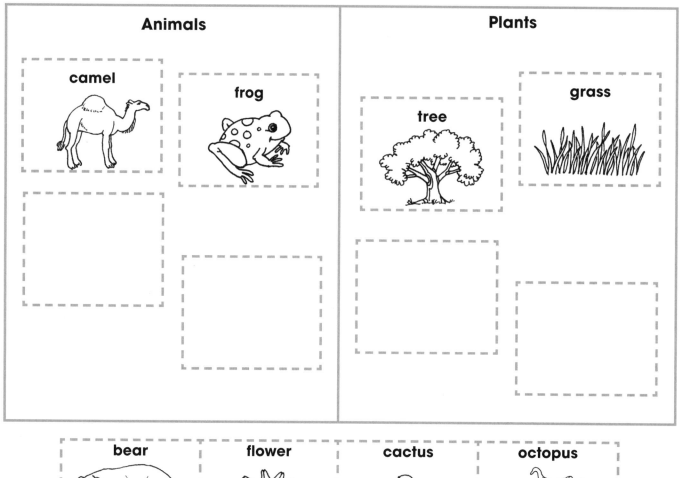

Listen to your teacher. Draw a picture.

An ocean has . . .

Overview   Science Words: Weather

Directions and Sample Answers for Activity Pages

Day 1	See "Provide a Real-World Example" below.
Day 2	Read aloud the title and directions. Guide students to identify the three types of weather. Help them cut out and identify the things we wear or use in different weather. Then help them glue each picture in the correct weather box.
Day 3	Read aloud the title and directions. Review the four seasons with students, pointing to each box as you say its name. Discuss the weather and temperature in each season, and show students how to circle **cold**, **cool**, **warm**, or **hot**. Finally, ask them to draw their favorite thing to do in each season.
Day 4	Read aloud the title and directions. Direct students' attention to the first picture. **Ask:** *Does the rain fall up or down? Circle the answer.* Look at the next picture. **Ask:** *Is the snow going up or down? Circle the answer.* Finally **ask:** *Is the wind sending the kite up or down? Circle the answer.*
Day 5	Read aloud the title and directions. Allow time for students to complete the task. Afterward, meet individually with students to discuss their results. Use their responses to plan further instruction and review.

Provide a Real-World Example

◆ Invite the class to look outside. If it is sunny, **say:** *Today is sunny. I see the sun. The sun makes us feel warm.* Write the words **today**, **is**, **sun**, and **warm** on chart paper. Or, if it is rainy, you might **say:** *Today is windy. I feel the wind. The wind makes us feel cool.* Then write **wind** and **cool** on the chart paper. Adapt for the weather where you live.

◆ **Say:** *We use different words to describe the weather. Today we will practice using these words.*

◆ Hand out the Day 1 activity page. **Say:** *This is a weather wheel. Let's trace and write the weather words.* First point to the sun and say the word **sun**. Invite students to trace the word **sun**. Continue with each word on the weather wheel.

◆ After students complete the task, **ask:** *What is the weather like today?* Guide students to draw a circle around the picture that shows the weather today.

Weather

today

is

sun

warm

wind

cool

Name _____

Weather Wheel

Trace each word. Draw a circle around today's weather.

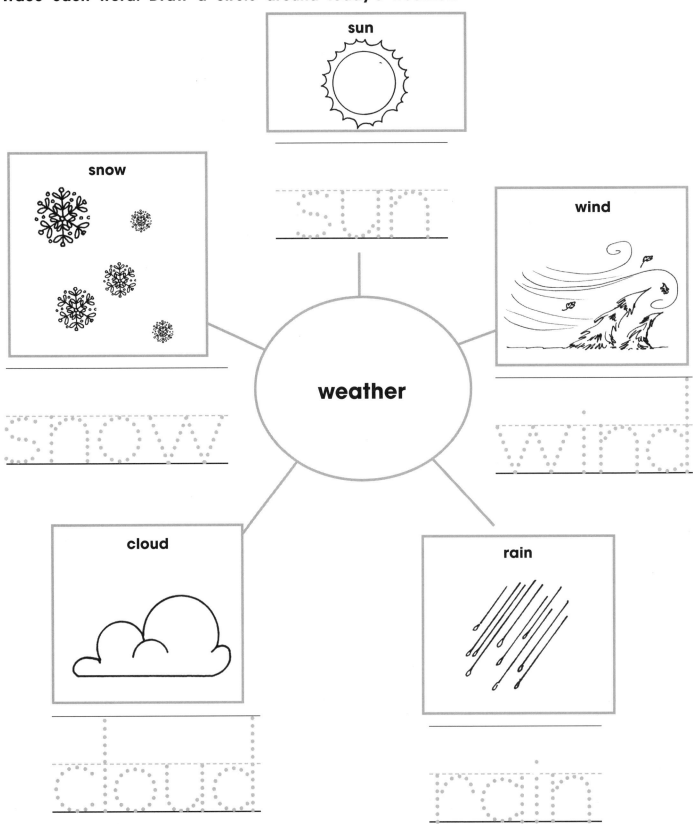

Weather Wear

Cut out the pictures. Glue the pictures in the right weather box.

 sun	 rain	 snow

umbrella	mittens	swimsuit
raincoat	sunglasses	scarf

Picture-Perfect Seasons

Circle the temperature in each season. Draw your favorite thing to do in each season.

winter	**spring**
cold cool warm hot	cold cool warm hot
summer	**fall**
cold cool warm hot	cold cool warm hot

Name _____

Up or Down?

Look at each picture. Listen to your teacher. Draw a circle around the answer.

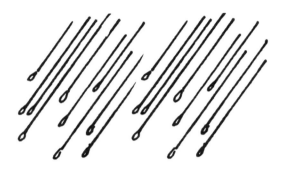

up   down

up   down

up   down

Name _____

Assessment

Draw a line to match each type of weather and activity.

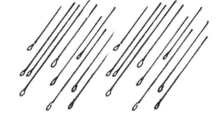

Unit 18 • Everyday Vocabulary Intervention Activities Grade K • ©2011 Newmark Learning, LLC

Overview   Math Words: Shapes and Numbers

Directions and Sample Answers for Activity Pages

Day 1	See "Provide a Real-World Example" below.
Day 2	Read aloud the title and directions. Help students cut out the cookies. Then help them match the cookies to the cookie jar with the same number and glue them on.
Day 3	Prepare for the game by writing these words on scraps of paper and putting them in a container: **one**, **four**, **six**, **ten**, **circle**, **rectangle**, **square**, **triangle**. Read aloud the title and directions. Help students cut out the pictures and glue them on their Bingo card. When students are ready, pick words from the container and read aloud. Write each word on the board. Allow students time to mark their cards.
Day 4	Read aloud the title and directions. Help students read the numbers and color words in the key. You may have them draw a dot of color next to each number to help them identify which numbers go with which colors. Then have students color in the rainbow.
Day 5	Read aloud the title and directions for the first task. Allow time for students to complete the first task. Then read aloud the directions for the second task. Afterward, meet individually with students to discuss their results. Use their responses to plan further instruction and review.

Provide a Real-World Example

♦ Stack three books on your desk so students can see. **Ask:** *How many books are in the pile?* (Allow responses.) **Say:** *Yes! There are three books in the pile.* Count out the books one at a time. Then write the word **three** on chart paper.

♦ Hold up one of the books. **Say:** *This book is a rectangle.* Point to each of the book's sides as you **say:** *A rectangle has four sides. Two sides are long and two are short.* Write **four** and **rectangle** on the chart paper. **Say:** *This week we will explore number and shape words.*

♦ Hand out the Day 1 activity page. Draw attention to the pizza pie. **Say:** *This pizza pie has six slices. Let's color the pizza pie. Let's trace the word* **six**. **Ask:** *Is the pizza pie a circle or a square?* (Allow responses.) Then **say:** *Yes! The pizza pie is a circle. Let's draw a circle around the word* **circle**.

♦ Draw attention to the two slices of pizza. **Say:** *Here are two slices of pizza. Let's color the slices. Let's trace the word* **two**. **Ask:** *What shape is a slice of pizza: a square or a triangle?* (Allow responses.) Then **say:** *Yes! A slice is a triangle. Let's draw a circle around the word* **triangle** *on the board.*
Now focus on the third picture. **Say:** *Here is one pizza box. Let's color the box. Let's trace the word* **one**. **Ask:** *What shape is the box: a circle or a square?* Then **say:** *Yes! The box is a square. Let's draw a circle around the word* **square**.

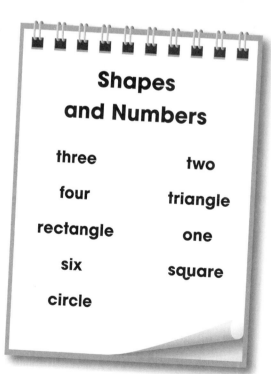

Shapes and Numbers

three   two

four   triangle

rectangle   one

six   square

circle

Pizza Parlor

Listen to your teacher. Color the pictures. Trace the words. Circle the shapes.

A pizza pie is a ○ circle ▢ square .

_____

six

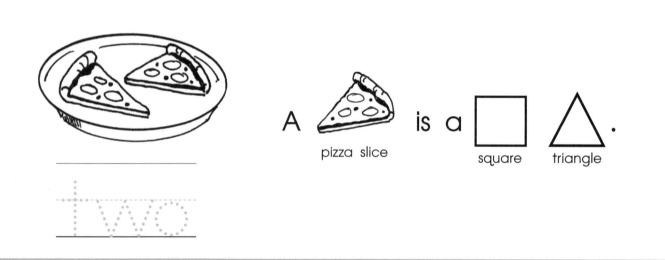

A pizza slice is a ▢ square △ triangle .

_____

two

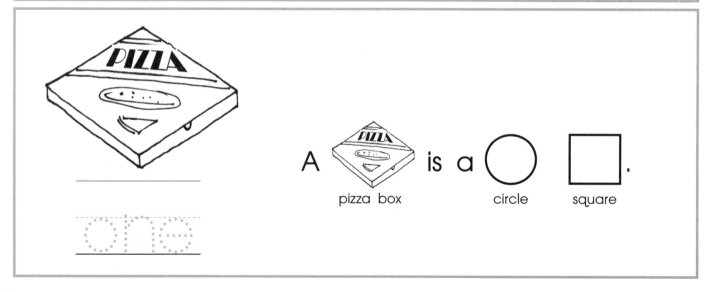

A pizza box is a ○ circle ▢ square .

_____

one

Cookie Jar

Cut out the cookies. Glue the cookies in the jar that has the same number on it.

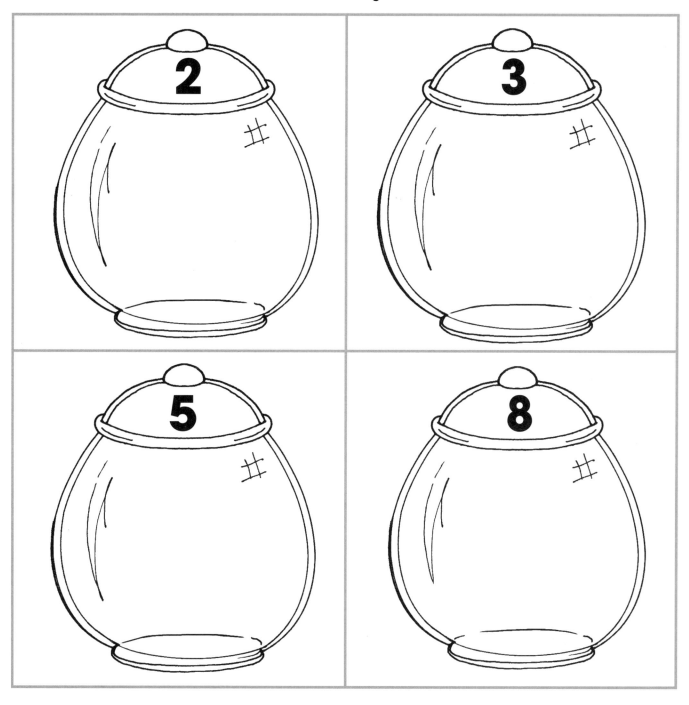

Shapes and Numbers Bingo

Cut out the shapes and numbers. Glue them onto your Bingo card.
Listen to the words your teacher calls out. Put an X on that shape or number.
Three in a row wins Bingo!

	Free Space	

one 1	four 4	six 6	ten 10
circle	rectangle	square	triangle

Name _____

Color-a-Rainbow

Use the color key to color the rainbow.

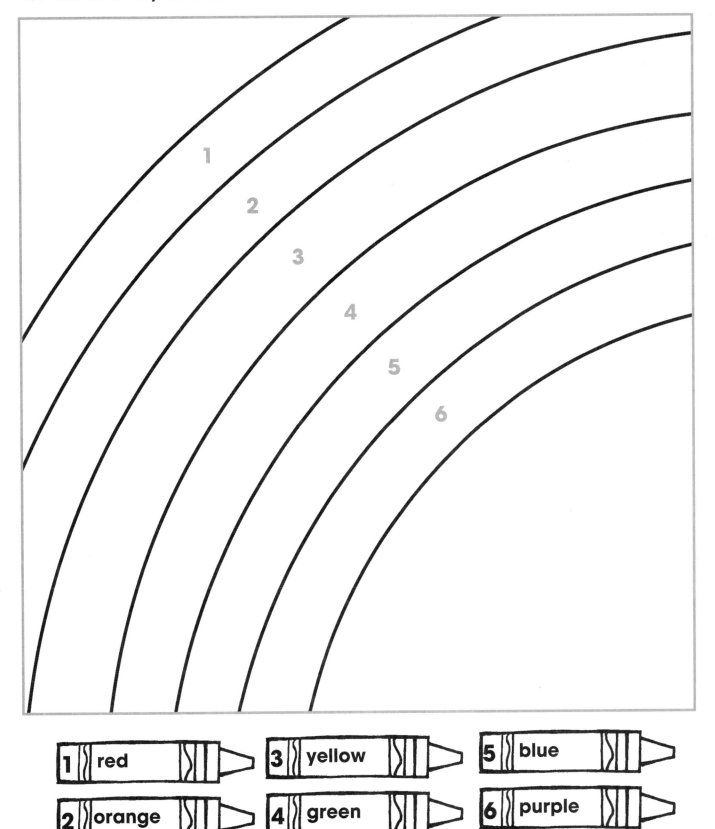

| 1 | red | 3 | yellow | 5 | blue |
| 2 | orange | 4 | green | 6 | purple |

Assessment

Draw a line to match the balloons to a number.

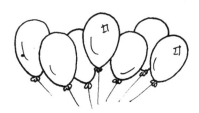

5
five

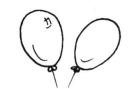

7
seven

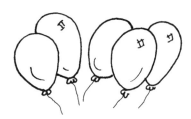

2
two

Draw a line to match each object with its shape.

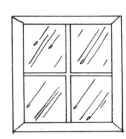

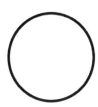

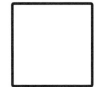

Overview Math Words: Comparing

Directions and Sample Answers for Activity Pages

Day 1	See "Provide a Real-World Example" below.
Day 2	Read aloud the title and directions. Look at each pair. Help students count and read the numbers in the rebus. Guide students to color the picture that shows less.
Day 3	Read aloud the title and directions. Help students count. Then guide them to identify the picture that shows more than the big picture in each section. Help students draw a circle around the pictures that show more.
Day 4	Read aloud the title and directions. Help students cut out and identify the pictures. Model how to glue big things under Billy and little things under Lilly.
Day 5	Read aloud the title and directions. Allow time for students to complete the task. Afterward, meet individually with students to discuss their results. Use their responses to plan further instruction and review.

Provide a Real-World Example

◆ Display two glasses of water. Fill one to the top. Fill the other less than halfway. Point to the full glass and **say:** *This glass has more water.* Write **more** on chart paper. Point to the glass with less water. **Say:** *This glass has less water.* Write **less** on the chart paper. **Say:** *We use the words **more** and **less** to compare the amounts of things.*

◆ Invite a volunteer to stand next to you. Point to yourself and **say:** *I am big.* Write **big** on the chart paper. Then point to the student and **say:** *You are little.* Write **little** on the chart paper. **Say:** *We use the words **big** and **little** to compare the sizes of things. This week we will practice using words that compare.*

◆ Hand out the Day 1 activity page. **Say:** *Welcome to the circus! Look at the two children eating cotton candy. The girl has more cotton candy than the boy. Let's trace the word **more***. Then **say:** *The boy has less cotton candy. Let's trace the word **less***. Now draw students' attention to the elephant. **Say:** *An elephant is a big animal. Let's trace the word **big***. Now focus on the mouse. **Say:** *A mouse is little. Let's trace the word **little***.

◆ Direct attention to the two ice cream cones. Count aloud the scoops on each cone. **Ask:** *Which cone has more scoops? Let's color in the ice cream cone that has more scoops.*

Comparing Words

more

less

big

little

Circus Fun

Look at the pictures. Trace the words.

more   less

big   little

Count the scoops in both cones. Color in the cone that has more.

Which Is Less?

Look at each pair. Color in the picture that shows less.

one

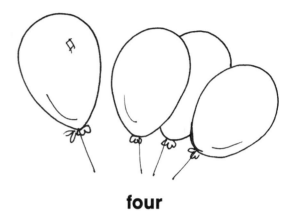

four

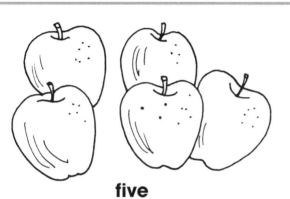

five

three

seven

two

six

eight

Name _____

Which Is More?

Look at the pictures. In each box, draw a circle around the picture that shows more than the big picture.

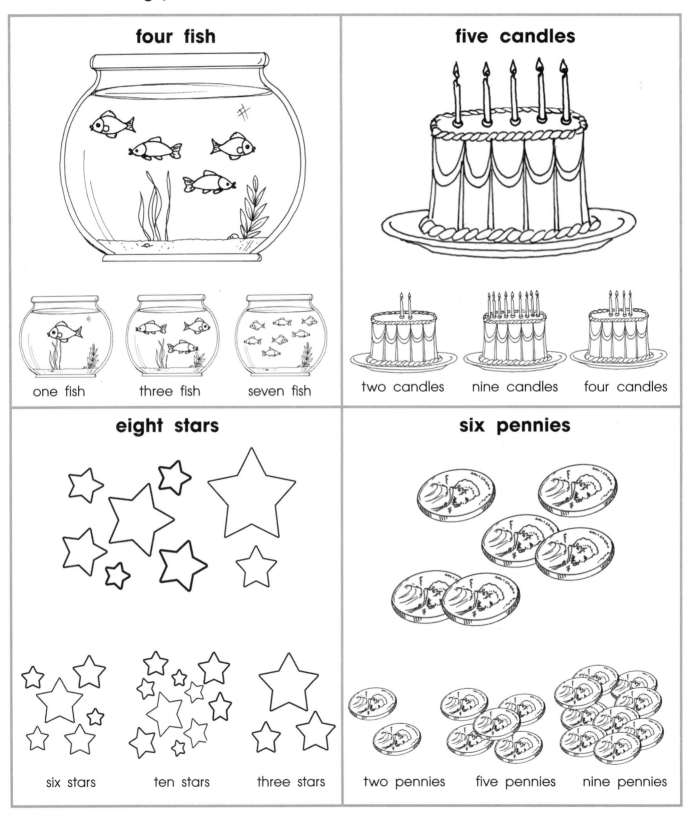

Name _____

Big Billy and Little Lilly

Billy and Lilly's things got mixed up. Billy's things are big. Lilly's things are little.
Cut out the pictures. Glue the big things under Billy. Glue the little things under Lilly.

Little Lilly	Big Billy

big hat	little hat	big kite	little kite	big boots

little boots	big ball	little ball	big bear	little bear

Day 5 • Comparing Words

Name _____

Assessment

Listen to your teacher. Circle the right answer.

Which is big?

Which is little?

Which is more?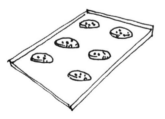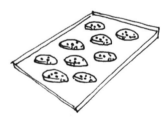

Which is less?

Unit 20 • Everyday Vocabulary Intervention Activities Grade K • ©2011 Newmark Learning, LLC

Notes

Notes

Everyday Vocabulary Intervention Activities Grade K • ©2011 Newmark Learning, LLC